ideals
THANKSGIVING

More Than 50 Years of Celebrating Life's Most Treasured Moments

Vol. 52, No. 7

"God has two dwellings: one in heaven,
And the other in meek and thankful hearts."
—*Izaak Walton*

IDEALS—Vol. 52, No. 7 November MCMXCV IDEALS (ISSN 0019-137X) is published eight times a year: February, March, May, June, August, September, November, December by IDEALS PUBLICATIONS INCORPORATED, 535 Metroplex Drive, Suite 250, Nashville, TN 37211. Second-class postage paid at Nashville, Tennessee, and additional mailing offices. Copyright © MCMXCV by IDEALS PUBLICATIONS INCORPORATED. POSTMASTER: Send address changes to Ideals, PO Box 305300, Nashville, TN 37230. All rights reserved. Title IDEALS registered U.S. Patent Office.

SINGLE ISSUE—U.S. $5.95 USD; Higher in Canada
ONE-YEAR SUBSCRIPTION—8 issues—U.S. $19.95 USD; Canada $36.00 CDN (incl. GST and shipping); Foreign $25.95 USD
TWO-YEAR SUBSCRIPTION—16 issues—U.S. $35.95 USD; Canada $66.50 CDN (incl. GST and shipping); Foreign $47.95 USD

Printed and bound in USA by The Banta Company, Menasha, Wisconsin. Printed on Weyerhaeuser Husky.

The paper used in this publication meets the minimum requirements of American National Standard for Information Sciences—Permanence of Paper for Printed Library Materials, ANSI Z39.48-1984.

Unsolicited manuscripts will not be returned without a self-addressed, stamped envelope.

ISBN 0-8249-1131-8   GST 131903775

Cover Photo LAKE CHOCORUA, NEW HAMPSHIRE. William Johnson/Johnson's Photography.

Inside Front Cover STAY! AMERICAN COCKER SPANIEL. Robert K. Abbett, artist. Courtesy of the artist and Wild Wings, Inc., Lake City, Minnesota.

Inside Back Cover EVENING GRASS—CANADA GEESE. Dan Milbert, artist. Courtesy of the artist and Wild Wings, Inc., Lake City, Minnesota.

D1303244

The Thankful Season

Elisabeth Weaver Winstead

Thanksgiving is the splendor
    Of our treasured autumn scenes,
Golden corn and waving wheat
    With fruitful fields swept clean.

It's the memory of the fertile earth
    Turned for planting in the spring
And praise for the abundance
    That bright harvest days now bring.

Thanksgiving sends sweet messages
    That reach from heart to heart,
Uniting friends with loved ones
    Although they're miles apart.

It's an old but joyous feeling
    As our cheerful spirits mount,
For past efforts are rewarded
    With rich blessings left to count.

Thanksgiving Day is cherished
    In this great land where we live,
Reflected in our happy hearts
    And the grateful praise we give.

FARMLAND IN AUTUMN
Windsor County, Vermont
Steve Terrill Photography

It's That Time of Year

Kay Hoffman

Wild geese are flying overhead;
  The air is crisp and clear.
The last bright leaves are tumbling down,
  For it's that time of year.

The pungent smell of woodsmoke drifts
  From bonfires everywhere,
And squirrels darting to and fro
  Hide nuts in ample share.

Wagons filled with happy children
  Are seen on country lanes;

Older folk, in sweet nostalgia,
  Live childhood days again.

The flower beds now look forlorn;
  Jack Frost has passed our way.
With icy breath he seared the blooms
  That once were bright and gay.

A cozy fire is on the hearth;
  Dear friends have come to call.
Come let us share a cup of tea
  And say good-bye to fall.

BIRCH BIRDHOUSE
Dick Dietrich Photography

Overleaf Photograph
MT. HOOD
Gifford Pinchot National Forest, Washington
Steve Terrill Photography

Return to the Hills

Helen Jackson

Like a music of triumph and joy
    Sounds the roll of the wheels,
And the breath of the engine laughs out
    In loud chuckles and peals,
Like the laugh of a man that is glad
    Coming homeward at night.
I lean out of the window and nod
    To the left and the right
To my friends in the fields and the woods.
    Not a face do I miss;
The sweet asters and browned goldenrod,
    And that stray clematis,
Of all vagabonds dearest and best,
    In most seedy estate;

I am sure they all recognize me.
　　If I only could wait,
I should hear all the welcome which now
　　In their faces I read,
"O true lover of us and our kin,
　　We all bid thee Godspeed!"

> ## "In every thing give thanks."
>
> I Thessalonians 5:18a

An Old-Fashioned Thanksgiving

Helen Colwell Oakley

An old-fashioned Thanksgiving is best of all, I believe—one that's traditional all the way. But the early settlers did not always have the customary turkey for their Thanksgiving feast; they often enjoyed wild game, a plump roast of beef, or perhaps a savory roast of pork. With farm and country folks, a large roasting hen plucked from the family's flock was a popular choice. When I grew up on the farm many years ago, I well remember that my mother was famous for her roast chicken and dressing on our old-fashioned, traditional Thanksgiving Day celebrations. Reflecting upon my memories of those wonderful, long-ago Thanksgivings, I've discovered that I still follow many of the traditions that my family observed. My children in turn are following in my footsteps, as they too prefer a truly old-fashioned Thanksgiving.

While all holidays were much anticipated when I was a girl, Thanksgiving was special; for it signaled the beginning of a holiday season filled to overflowing with joyous tidings for one and all. Snowfalls seemed to come earlier back then, which provided "Currier-and-Ives" snow scenes round our countryside. Horse-drawn sleighs with tinkling bells dashed over the rural lanes as families and friends gathered together for a country-style Thanksgiving.

8

I remember in the olden days as Thanksgiving time approached, the barns were filled to the rafters, and the farmhouse had a larder that was heaped to the brim and running over as the bustle of harvest-time drew to a close. Then preparations for a bountiful Thanksgiving dinner were soon on the way. On the farm, most every dish for the feast came directly from the land, which made a farm family especially grateful on this day set aside to give thanks.

Our traditional Thanksgiving dinner has not changed much. Although we now order our turkey from the market, we have home-grown potatoes to provide fluffy mounds of mashed potatoes that are light as a cloud; a great hubbard squash to bake; cabbage, carrots, and green peppers for coleslaw; tomatoes and onions for relishes; grapes, blueberries, and apples for delicious, flaky, warm pies. Along with mincemeat pies and pumpkin pies fresh from the oven, the delicacies all seem to say "Thanksgiving is on the way!" so like in the days of old.

I believe it's only natural that we cling to our heritage and family traditions from years ago. Our reminiscent Thanksgiving is enjoyed to the fullest, for nothing can compare with the old-fashioned Thanksgiving flavor of days gone by.

SUNDAY MORNING. Sam Timm, artist.
Courtesy of the artist and Wild Wings, Inc., Lake City, Minnesota.

BITS & PIECES

In every thing by prayer and supplication with thanksgiving let your requests be made known unto God.

Philippians 4:6

I'm thankful for the common things
We often take for granted:
The sun, the rain, the birds, the trees,
Each flower that is planted.

M. Kathleen Haley

Not what we give, but what we share,
for the gift without the giver is bare.
Who gives himself with his alms feeds three—
himself, his hungering neighbor, and Me.

James Russell Lowell

Now thank we all our God
With heart and hand and voices;
Who wondrous things hath done,
In whom His world rejoices.

Martin Rinkart

Never lose an opportunity of seeing anything that is beautiful; for beauty is God's handwriting— a wayside sacrament. Welcome it in every fair face, in every sky, in every fair flower, and thank God for it as a cup of blessing.

Ralph Waldo Emerson

The year that is drawing toward its close
has been filled with the blessing of fruitful
fields and healthful skies—they are the gracious
gifts of the Most High God!

Abraham Lincoln

Not what we have, but what we enjoy,
constitutes our abundance.

J. Petit-Senn

Whether the motive which leads us to perform
an action is the love of neighbor or the love of God,
it is undeniable that pleasure enters into that motive.

Thomas Huxley

May silent thanks at least to God be given
with a full heart. Our thoughts are heard in heaven.

William Wordsworth

Autumn

Celia Lowell Doxtater

October's mist on dale and glen,
The frost nip in the air,
The azure blue sky overhead,
And brilliance everywhere.

The woodland hills and crested peaks,
Their foliage all ablaze
With reds and yellows, brown and gold
Against a purple haze.

The falling leaves—a golden shower—
Go whirling in the breeze
And pile up high against the wall
Beneath the great oak trees.

The sumac's torch of flaming red,
The maple's brown and gold
Against a bank of evergreen—
A glory to behold.

SUMAC
Fremont National Forest
Lake County, Oregon
Steve Terrill Photography

Country CHRONICLE

Lansing Christman

THE FLOWERS OF INDIAN SUMMER

Indian summer is a season by itself, brief though it is. No other time of the year is like it. With days that are mild and warm and hazy and serene, an unexpected Indian summer adds a special brilliance to autumn. I will long remember one particular autumn—the year that Indian summer came in early November and continued through Thanksgiving Day.

The haze that long ago November was like a bluish veil slipping down over the sides of the Blue Ridge Mountains and softly blanketing our foothills. I saw it in every direction, over valley and woodland, over orchard and field.

A chill edged into some of the sharp, clear, frosty nights. But when the sun came, it rapidly warmed the hills in time for my morning walk. How the webs of the gossamer glistened like silver when I walked in the fields! The slightest breeze sent them wavering as they floated through the air, the silken strands streaming down over my face and hands.

On Thanksgiving Day, flowers and bushes were in bloom. The golden dandelion and the white clover filled the lawn in abundance, and our dooryard bed of oxalis in its pure pink beauty was a welcome sight. Along the road I noticed the goldenrod and honeysuckle and Queen Anne's lace. In the fields, the purple, velvet-like flowers of the wild morning glory shone brilliantly in the sun.

Many surprises were in store, for some of the bushes and trees seemed to have been confused by the long period of warmth. Azaleas and roses were blossoming. The dooryard lilac was bearing miniature flowers that were densely clustered. Although the blossoms were nothing like the large clusters of spring, the delicate fragrance was definitely there. The catkins on the pussy willow seemed ready to burst, and a neighbor's roadside magnolia displayed two huge white and waxy blossoms in the warm sun.

During that unique time of unseasonal warmth, I was reminded of how nature will never cease to both delight and surprise me. While I enjoyed the continuous gifts of beauty that surrounded me, I gave my thanks for a special November when Indian summer was a part of Thanksgiving Day.

The author of two published books, Lansing Christman has been contributing to Ideals *for more than twenty years. Mr. Christman has also been published in several American, foreign, and braille anthologies. He lives in rural South Carolina.*

Overleaf Photograph
WOODLAND BEAUTY
Lincoln, Vermont
Ron Thomas/FPG

DRUMMOND'S GOLDENROD AND SPREADING ASTER
Solidago drummondii and *Aster patens*
Pacific, Missouri
R. Todd Davis Photography

Thanksgiving Day in the Country

John C. Bonser

There's a house in the country, long miles away
    And it seems like a lifetime ago,
Where our loved ones would gather on Thanksgiving Day
    Amid fields often feathered with snow.

We'd see chimney smoke curling up to the skies
    As we journeyed around the last bend;
The lights in the windows were welcoming eyes
    And the porch like the arm of a friend.

Then Mother and Father, a little more gray,
    Would gaily greet all at the door,
And the house would soon echo with children at play
    And a family together once more.

The aromas of turkey and dressing would fill
    The rooms with their glorious smell,
And we knew we would dine divinely until
    Our lives were replenished as well.

But first, heads were bowed for a moment of prayer
    That Father would lovingly give
In thanks for the blessings that all of us share
    In this land where we freely may live.

As the hours sped by and the flames flickered low
    From the logs in the warm fireplace,
We knew it was time to reluctantly go;
    And we kissed every dear person's face.

And Mother and Father would wave from the door
    As we honked last good-byes from our cars
Then started the drive to our own homes once more
    With our memories bright as the stars.

Now sometimes it seems that we actually see
    Those lights from their mansion above;
May the family of man some day be as free
    To feast at God's banquet of love!

Readers' Reflections

Haze on the Hill

The misty morning rises still
    Above each autumn-colored hill.
The heaven that was once bright blue
    Has taken on a grayish hue.
The fallen leaves have made a quilt
    Atop the moss the spring rain built.

And every bird and forest deer
    Is planning for the winter near.
Then as I look I feel the chill
    Of misty hazes on the hill;
For soon I know will come the snow
    That, like the mist, will drift and blow.

Joan Stephen
Portville, New York

Autumn Leaves

The autumn leaves are falling;
    There's crispness in the air.
I marvel at God's handiwork
    He has given us to share.

The leaves they keep on swirling
    As round and round they go—
Shades from a golden sunset,
    Their beauty all aglow.

I'm like a child at Christmas;
    I cease to understand

The meaning of each twirling leaf
    And the beauty of our land.

Then I close my eyes, envisioning leaves
    As different people we meet each day,
Their lives entwining ours,
    Circling close then flying away.

How majestic is His creation—
    People and leaves of every race and hue.
And kneeling down with childlike faith,
    I give thanks for another autumn view.

Joanna Boles
Garden City, Kansas

Editor's Note: Readers are invited to submit unpublished, original poetry for possible publication in future issues of Ideals. *Please send typed copies only; manuscripts will not be returned. Writers receive $10 for each published submission. Send material to* Readers' Reflections, Ideals Publications Inc., 535 Metroplex Drive, Suite 250, Nashville, Tennessee 37211.

A Prayer for Thanksgiving

We give our thanks, dear Lord, to You
    This special time of year
For blessing us with lives so full
    Of love and friends so dear;

For teaching us to share our lives
    With others having less;
And giving those who are in need
    Of love and tenderness.

You show us how to clothe and feed
    The hungry and the cold,
With help from others in our town
    Whose hearts are made of gold.

So thank You, Lord, for giving us
    The patience and the heart
To care for those You send our way
    Who need a helping start.

Kathleen Pidwell
Cuyahoga Falls, Ohio

Autumn Song

Autumn sings a song of haze,
    Cool and wispy, washed with maize.
Soft and whispering moments still,
    Then branches bending, sent with chill.
Misty morning, sunset bright,
    Dusty twilight turned to night.
Each passing day that's filled with cold,
    While Autumn sings, her leaves turn gold.

Brenda Roeske
Egg Harbor, New Jersey

Waiting for Winter

Autumn blushes forth with shades of rosy red;
    Pine needles slumber in my flower bed.
Whirlwinds of leaves swirl around my toes,
    Puffy clouds of smoke tickling my nose.
Arctic breezes whisper to my furry friends,
    Telling bedtime stories as the sleep begins.

Patti Schleeter
Grand Haven, Michigan

My Everyday Thanksgiving

Ardis Rittenhouse

The morning sun that awakens me
Makes me thankful I can see.
Loved ones' voices each so dear
Make me thankful I can hear.
Health and strength that get me through
Make me thankful for what I can do.
Faith that does not let me stray
Makes me thankful for each day.
A mind that reasons and is fair
Makes me thankful that I care.
A heart that accepts help from above
Makes me thankful for God's love.

Thank you for
    the sunset that sings us to sleep,
    the darkness that blankets our rest,
    the sunrise that yanks off the covers,
    the light that reveals our next step.
          —Evelyn Bence

TENNESSEE CHAPEL
Maryville, Tennessee
Gene Ahrens Photography

Prairie Country

Craig E. Sathoff

The prairie country nurtured me
   When I was just a boy.
Within its arms it strengthened me
   With fruitfulness and joy.

The prairie land is level land
   Where crops grow strong and tall,
Where harvests are abundant,
   And where calm lies over all.

It used to be that windmills
   Were the signposts of the land;
For every place a mill was seen,
   There too a farm would stand.

But with the passing of the years,
   The windmills ceased to be,
And elevators filled with grain
   Are now the signs we see.

The prairie land is changing land;
   The seasons come on rough.
The twisters, hails, and blizzards
   Help to make a farmer tough.

But still the prairie knows such calm
   That with return of spring,
A sacred hush, a gentle touch,
   Envelopes everything.

The prairie land is vital land,
   Aglow with life and health—
A knowing land, a growing land,
   A source of inner wealth.

TRAVELER'S Diary

Heather R. McArthur

VERMILIONVILLE CAJUN VILLAGE CHURCH. Lafayette, Louisiana. John Elk III Photography.

THE ACADIAN VILLAGES OF LOUISIANA

I grew up in Baton Rouge, Louisiana, where my mother often served *boudin*, crawfish *étouffée*, and shrimp bisque. I began learning to speak French in the first grade, and my Girl Scouts troop took field trips to places such as the Evangeline Oak in St. Martinville and the Acadian Village on the outskirts of Lafayette. It was at this re-creation of a typical Cajun community that I first learned about the Acadians, or Cajuns, who lived on the bayous of South Louisiana where they fished for a living and heartily maintained their creed *"laissez les bons temps rouler!"* (let the good times roll!). Not until recently did I rediscover the origins of this fascinating culture and once again venture to Lafayette, the unofficial capital of Acadiana.

In 1604, fifteen years before the *Mayflower* made its passage across the Atlantic Ocean, thousands of French Catholics established their first permanent colony in Acadie, or modern day Nova Scotia. Some eighteen thousand French immigrants lived peacefully until the region fell into British hands in 1713. Refusing to pledge allegiance to the British crown and the Anglican church, the Acadians were forced to flee southward by Governor Charles Lawrence in 1755. During the Grand Derangement, families were separated, and nearly half lost their lives due to harsh weather conditions. It was during this time that the legend of Evangeline was born. Henry Wadsworth Longfellow immortalized the legend in his epic poem that told of Evangeline, the young Acadian maiden who was separated from her beloved fiance by the 1755 exile.

The Acadians who survived the expulsion were met with much hostility as they approached ports along the Eastern seaboard of North America. Finally, in 1784, after nearly thirty years of nomadic interludes, the King of Spain permitted the exiles to settle in South Louisiana. Today, the descendants of those "pilgrims" constitute the largest French-speaking minority in the United States. Modern-day "Cajuns" (a distortion of *Acadian*, or *Cadien*) reside in the twenty-two parish area surrounding Lafayette, Louisiana, known as Acadiana and cling tightly to their traditional French heritage. I became one of the many visitors that gather underneath live oak trees filled with Spanish moss to experience traditional Cajun life.

My first stop was the original Acadian Village, a folk-life museum featuring period homes from the nineteenth century that have been restored and carefully furnished with authentic, native Louisiana antiques. Surrounded by ten acres of gardens and woodland, the quaint village is situated on a small bayou and includes a replica of a village store and chapel. The traditional Acadian cottage was raised on piers and included an outdoor stairway in an attempt to ventilate stuffy rooms and to prevent flooding in the spring. This Acadian cottage design is often replicated today in modern, suburban neighborhoods.

VILLAGE WEAVER. Vermilionville Cajun Village. Lafayette, Louisiana. John Elk III Photography.

I traveled on to Vermilionville, a twenty-three-acre living history museum located on Bayou Vermilion. Costumed guides and interpreters led me along the cypress-shaded paths between period homes dating from 1765 to 1890. As I approached the museum, I could hear live Cajun music coming from inside. Costumed hosts deftly demonstrated the "Cajun two-step," and I found myself tapping my feet to the accordion and washboard sound. Cajun culinary specialities are prepared on the premises, and I eagerly sampled gumbo, crawfish tails, and spicy *andouille* sausage. The distinct Cajun cuisine is the result of French influences and the Cajuns' dependence on waterways that supported a wide variety of fish and wildlife.

The bayou lifestyle of the Cajuns resulted in geographical and cultural isolation. They were forced to survive independently from Anglo settlements farther to the east and thus maintained their unique linguistic and ethnic identities. The rigors of the original Cajuns' everyday life are exhibited today by the bilingual guides' dexterity at the loom, where bed linens and clothing were all homespun. Descendants of original Acadians demonstrate the potter's wheel and the tools of the silversmith, all central to pioneer living, while boatbuilders work diligently to shape the shallow canoes called *pirogues* that were used as transportation along the narrow bayou inlets of South Louisiana. I was even given the chance to cross the bayou in a genuine *pirogue*, dodging cypress knobs and sleepy alligators, to *La Chapelle des Attakapas*, a chapel modeled after the first Cajun church.

After a visit to the Acadian Village and Vermilionville, I am left with a sense of the unique lifestyle of the early Cajuns. I was able to pass through the heart of Acadiana and directly experience the architecture, food, and language of a formerly isolated culture. Now that the Cajun culture is accessible to others, people worldwide are able to experience and enjoy the Cajuns' distinct music, architecture, and cooking. But my trip to the Acadian Villages has taught me that the true Cajun heritage is much more than spicy delicacies and festive bands; it is marked by strength, faith, and endurance during times of difficulty and an ever-present *joie de vivre*.

A native of Louisiana, Heather R. McArthur is a recent graduate of Vanderbilt University, where she majored in religious studies. She worked as Ideals' editorial intern during her senior year and dedicates much of her free time to volunteer work.

Thank God Every Morning

Charles Kingsley

Thank God every morning when you get up that you have something to do that day which must be done, whether you like it or not. Being forced to work and forced to do your best will breed in you temperance and self-control, diligence and strength of will, cheerfulness and content, and a hundred virtues which the idle will never know.

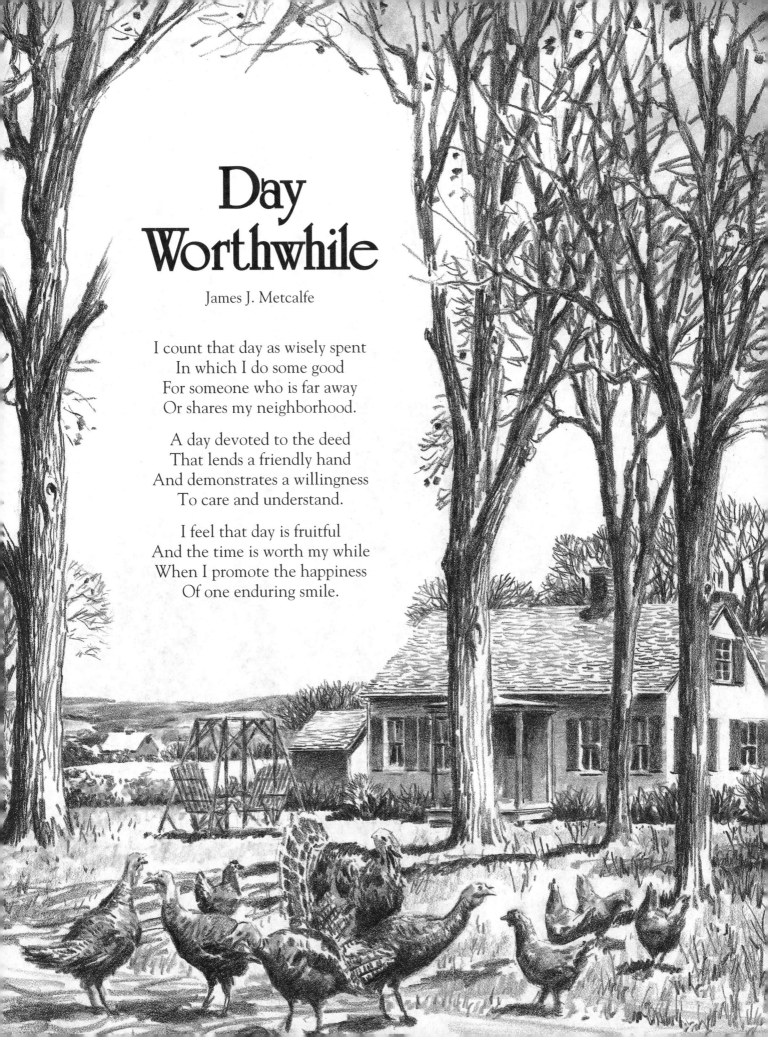

Day Worthwhile

James J. Metcalfe

I count that day as wisely spent
In which I do some good
For someone who is far away
Or shares my neighborhood.

A day devoted to the deed
That lends a friendly hand
And demonstrates a willingness
To care and understand.

I feel that day is fruitful
And the time is worth my while
When I promote the happiness
Of one enduring smile.

I Have Planted a Cornfield

Edith Lombard Squires

I have planted a cornfield to hold the sun,
And to hang the autumn mists upon,
And to store in its shocks a song of gold—
All that the Spring and Summer have told.

The pricking blade with its earthen hilt,
This mighty highway the sun has built,
The tented ranks of Indian lore
That hold in their hearts earth's golden store.

Blackbirds and grackles have heard the call
Each misty morning of early fall;
They've paid with the beauty of soaring flight
For this bounty of ear—their ancient right.

I have planted a cornfield, an age-old task,
But all that the heart of man could ask—
Birth and earth's springtime, youth's hot sun,
And the golden kernels of life new won.

THROUGH MY WINDOW

Pamela Kennedy

Art by Russ Flint

A THANKSGIVING PAGEANT TO REMEMBER

I had been asked to organize the annual Thanksgiving program at my son's preschool; and since he was my first child, I was naive enough to see the request as an honor. The teacher, delighted with my enthusiasm and the realization she had a novice in the job, gave me free rein to plan whatever I liked to help the children "understand the true meaning of Thanksgiving." Given my natural bent towards the dramatic, I decided to orchestrate a pageant, complete with Indians, Pilgrims, and a finale that included a feast prepared by the children themselves. As I ran over the details of my plan with the teacher, I failed to catch the irony in her voice when she smiled and said, "I just know this year our program will be truly memorable."

I wanted to help the children understand the context of the first Thanksgiving; I wanted to fill them with awe at the courage of their forefathers and to imbue them with respect for the Native Americans who encouraged and aided the struggling immigrants. I spent hours in the library researching the events at Plymouth and brought storybooks about the plight of the Pilgrims to share with the children.

In early November, I spent an afternoon with the class, telling them about Squanto and William Bradford and the fierce winter and the hopelessness faced by the little band of Pilgrims. Then I told them about the helpfulness and cooperation between the Wampanoags and the settlers and finally about the Thanksgiving feast they all shared. The children listened attentively and seemed delighted with the prospect of reenacting the story. I was thrilled.

"Okay, who would like to be an Indian?" I asked. All the boys raised their hands. "We can't have all of you be Indians! We need some men Pilgrims too."

"They dressed funny," offered one, "and they had ponytails."

"Yeah, and they lived in houses. The Indians got to camp out and carry spears and knives and kill stuff."

I assured them that no one in our pageant was going to carry a knife or "kill stuff."

"Boring," chorused the discontented young males.

"Let's talk about the feast," I countered. "We'll worry about who's who later." I read aloud the list of food items noted in the journals of some of the participants at the first Thanksgiving.

"Eels?!!" "Yuck!" "Gross!" "No way am I eating clams." "I think I'm allergic to squash." "I had deer once and it made me throw up." The chorus of naysayers drowned me out.

"We don't have to eat the same exact things. We could pretend," I suggested. "What do you think we should have?"

"Hot dogs!" "Pizza!" "Cheeseburgers!" "Tacos!"

I looked at the bemused teacher, sitting at the back of the room, obviously enjoying the whole scene.

After some time, we decided to compromise on apple juice, popcorn, and pumpkin pie; and I relented and let all the boys be Indians and carry knives made of cardboard. The girls agreed to be Pilgrims "and pretend all the men are inside with bad colds." It wasn't quite what I had planned, but still I held out hope that the "true meaning of Thanksgiving" could be salvaged.

The morning of the pageant, the class assembled in the school kitchen to make the "feast." As we worked, I thought it might just be simpler to cook over an open fire in sub-zero temperatures in seventeenth-century New England.

Everyone on our apple juice committee felt compelled to add a personal can of water to the frozen concentrate. It came out pale and tasteless. When we popped the corn, someone shoved the bowl at the crucial moment, and the air popper spewed its contents all over the table and floor, sending the children shrieking with laughter as they tried to catch the errant kernels. The pie-making Pilgrims had an argument over who was going to break the eggs, and someone dropped the whole carton. After the tears and slime were mopped up, I was the first one ready for a nap when the teacher suggested it was quiet time.

Refreshed after our short break, I helped my little braves don their fringed paper-bag vests and pinned white caps and collars on the Pilgrim girls. As I read the account of the first Thanksgiving, the children pantomimed their parts dutifully, then gathered in a big circle on the floor to enjoy their feast. While sticky fingers dunked popcorn in cups of watery apple juice and the Wampanoags carved slivers of pie with cardboard knives, the teacher asked each child to share something for which he or she was thankful. One by one, the children mentioned family or pets or a special toy. But the comment that I will always cherish came from a little boy who announced, "I'm thankful Mithuth Kennedy helped uth have a real Thankthgiving, and I didn't have to dreth up like a Pilgrim and eat eelth and clamth." A chorus of "Eeewws!" affirmed his gratitude.

Later, as I cleaned the pumpkin pie off my slacks and sweater, I smiled as I thought of something else for which to give thanks. Next year I would be smart enough to decline the honor of preparing the Thanksgiving program!

Pamela Kennedy is a freelance writer of short stories, articles, essays, and children's books. Wife of a naval officer and mother of three children, she has made her home on both U.S. coasts and currently resides in Honolulu, Hawaii. She draws her material from her own experiences and memories, adding highlights from her imagination to enhance the story.

A Tree

Carolyn J. Tinkle

There are few greater beauties
    That one could hope to see
Than the silent strong formation
    Of the old majestic tree.

Its strength is in its roots;
    Its arms reach toward the sky.
Its leaves rustle so gently
    As the soft wind whispers by.

It offers shade to those who rest
    Beneath its spreading boughs;
Lovers carve initialed hearts,
    Exchanging secret vows.

Many artists are inspired
    By beauty they perceive

While contemplating nature
    Beneath its lacy leaves.

Birds make homes on sturdy limbs,
    Protected from the night;
Squirrels cavorting round its trunk
    Give watchers such delight.

Children's fantasies expand
    As they climb up and play;
Swings attached to higher limbs
    Bring joy each autumn day.

Its wood is used for shelter,
    For paper, books, and toys;
Another of God's blessings
    Gives help as well as joy.

FOR THE CHILDREN

Artwork by Russ Flint

WE THANK THEE

Author Unknown

For mothers' love and fathers' care,
For brothers strong and sisters fair,
For love at home and here each day,
For guidance lest we go astray,
    Father in heaven, we thank Thee.

For flowers that bloom about our feet,
For tender grass, so fresh, so sweet,
For song of bird and hum of bee,
For all things fair we hear or see,
    Father in heaven, we thank Thee.

For blue of stream and blue of sky,
For pleasant shade of branches high,
For fragrant air and cooling breeze,
For beauty of the blooming trees,
    Father in heaven, we thank Thee.

The unique perspective of Russ Flint's artistic style has made him a favorite of Ideals *readers for many years. A resident of California and father of four, Russ Flint has illustrated a children's Bible and many other books.*

Thanksgiving Day

Lydia Maria Child

Over the river and through the wood,
To Grandfather's house we go;
    The horse knows the way
    To carry the sleigh
Through the white and drifted snow.

Over the river and through the wood—
Oh, how the wind does blow!
    It stings the toes
    And bites the nose
As over the ground we go.

Over the river and through the wood,
To have a first-rate play.
    Hear the bells ring,
    "Ting-a-ling-ding!"
Hurrah for Thanksgiving Day!

Over the river and through the wood,
Trot fast, my dapple-gray!
    Spring over the ground
    Like a hunting hound!
For this is Thanksgiving Day.

Over the river and through the wood,
And straight through the barnyard gate.
    We seem to go
    Extremely slow—
It is so hard to wait!

Over the river and through the wood—
Now Grandmother's cap I spy!
    Hurrah for the fun!
    Is the pudding done?
Hurrah for the pumpkin pie!

Ideals'
Family Recipes

Favorite Recipes from the Ideals Family of Readers

Editor's Note: Please send us your best-loved recipes! Mail a typed copy of the recipe along with your name, address, and telephone number to Ideals magazine, ATTN: Recipes, P.O. Box 305300, Nashville, Tennessee 37230. We will pay $10 for each recipe used. Recipes cannot be returned.

PILGRIM'S DELIGHT PUMPKIN PIE

Soak 3 ounces pecan pieces in ½ cup maple syrup for one hour. Pour the pecan mixture into a 9-inch unbaked pastry shell, pressing the pecans firmly into the shell.

Beat one 8-ounce package softened cream cheese with an electric mixer until creamy. Add ¼ cup granulated sugar and ½ teaspoon vanilla; beat until light and fluffy. Add 1 egg; beat until smooth. Pour cream cheese mixture over the pecan mixture; chill at least 2 hours.

Preheat oven to 350° F. Combine 1¼ cups cooked, mashed pumpkin; 1 cup evaporated milk; ½ cup granulated sugar; 2 eggs (slightly beaten); 1 teaspoon ground cinnamon; ¼ teaspoon ground nutmeg; and a dash of salt. Beat until smooth. Carefully spoon mixture over the cream cheese and pecan mixtures in the pie shell. Bake 1 hour. Brush with maple syrup and garnish with pecan halves. Makes 8 servings.

Michaele S. Russell
Greenwood, Delaware

Holiday Walnut Pie

Preheat oven to 400° F. In a large mixing bowl, lightly beat 3 eggs. Stir in 1 cup granulated sugar, 2 tablespoons all-purpose flour, 1 cup light corn syrup, 2 tablespoons melted butter, and 1 teaspoon vanilla. Mix well.

To prevent over-browning, cover the edge of an unbaked, 9-inch pastry shell with foil. Place the shell on the oven rack in the lower third of the oven and pour mixture into the shell. Arrange 1½ cups large pieces of English walnuts over the top. Bake at 400° F for 15 minutes. Reduce oven temperature to 350° F and bake an additional 15 minutes. Remove foil and bake 20 to 30 minutes more or until center appears set. Cool completely before serving. Makes 8 servings.

Florence Heinecke
Ripon, Wisconsin

Chocolate-Pecan Pie

Preheat oven to 350° F. In a large mixing bowl, lightly beat 3 eggs with a wire whisk. Stir in 1 cup light corn syrup, ½ cup granulated sugar, and ⅓ cup melted margarine or butter. Mix well. Stir in 1 cup pecan halves.

To prevent over-browning, cover the edge of an unbaked, 9-inch pastry shell with foil. Sprinkle ½ cup semisweet chocolate pieces over the bottom of the shell. After placing the pie pan on the oven rack, pour the filling into the shell.

Bake 25 minutes. Remove foil and bake 20 to 25 minutes more or until a toothpick comes out clean. Makes 8 servings.

Olive Jordan
Corona, California

Peanut Butter Pie

In a large bowl, combine ½ cup smooth peanut butter with one 8-ounce package softened cream cheese. Blend well with an electric mixer until light and fluffy. Add 1 cup confectioner's sugar and blend well. Gradually add ½ cup milk, mixing well on high until mixture thickens. Fold in one 8-ounce container of non-dairy whipped topping. Spread mixture into a 9-inch graham cracker pie shell; cover and freeze. Makes 6 to 8 servings.

Phyllis M. Peters
Three Rivers, Michigan

50 YEARS AGO

A RUSSIAN SOLDIER HUGS AN AMERICAN SOLDIER. Germany, May 1945. Photograph U.S. Signal Corps, courtesy of the National Archives.

TOWARD A DYNAMIC THANKSGIVING

It is with mixed emotions that Americans enter this Thanksgiving season. On the one hand, we are deeply grateful for the end of hostilities. On the other, we realize that problems of surpassing gravity lie ahead. And as we express our deep and reverent gratitude for perils passed and dangers destroyed, we pray for understanding and wisdom with which to find our way clearly through the mists of the future.

And so today it is prudent for us to make our Thanksgiving observance much more than grati-tude for dangers overcome. We must make our gratitude dynamic. Many of us have learned the healing and regenerating power of gratitude. Now is the time to apply that lesson. For this Thanksgiving points ahead, if ever one did, to the need of alertness to future dangers, of responsibility for world relationships, and to the imperative necessity that the affairs of men be lifted out of their materialistic framework. Material force has overrun itself. The only possible basis of peace is agreement. And agreement is a mental state, a thing of the spirit and the understanding. Gratitude can pave the way to agreement.

A good way for Americans to begin to observe this Thanksgiving—if they wish to enjoy their turkeys—is to see that they have done everything in their power to share their well-being with millions in need in the less bountifully supplied nations. It is not at all clear that we are doing all we can to feed and clothe the needy in Europe. Every bit of aid that can be shipped to the needy nations should be sent. This is the first step in making our gratitude dynamic.

The second and closely kindred step is the acceptance of our world responsibilities. For what are we most grateful this year? For the end of hostilities, no doubt. How did hostilities come to end? To what do we owe this victory? We owe it, of course, to a whole chain of factors: the heroic sacrifices of our Allies when the outlook seemed darkest; the unflagging resistance of the invaded people—all this under God's protecting care for the right. But the victory would never have been won if America had not awakened to its world relationships. Our mobilization of manpower and industry, of talent and resources and sacrifices, was a vital factor. Shall we now throw it all away by seeking to forget or deny our responsibilities?

PICCADILLY CIRCUS, LONDON. May 8, 1945.
Photograph courtesy of the National Archives.

Only if America carries over into the peace, and retains unremittingly, the same sense of teamwork and world effort which we showed during the war, can we hope to win the peace. And unless the peace is won, our gratitude today will be a mockery and a sham. We must look ahead. A small part of our task has been achieved—a small part only. The dangers of the present and the future are no less acute than the dangers we faced during the war, for they are more subtle and disguised. Fear will not protect us from the effects of fear. But awakening and awareness can open the way to protection. We must awaken to these threats which endanger humankind and take speedy and effective action.

What action? A determination to prevent all war. The prevention cannot come, we now know, from multiplications of our own weapons of war. War can be prevented only by eliminating fear and the causes of fear and by establishing and maintaining universal good will.

It takes two to make enmity, two to create ill will. If Americans wish to make their gratitude dynamic, if we wish to retain the blessings which so abundantly pour in upon us at this season of Thanksgiving, then we must begin to actively demonstrate good will. We can first do this by helping the starving and freezing of the world. We can do it by helping in the restoration of the world economy through loans and grants and other practical aid. We can do it by making an intensive effort to see our own actions as others see us.

Not the least of our needs is to demonstrate good will at home, in the relations of worker and employer. The real interests of both are identical: the achievement of reconversion, full employment, and large-scale production at prices which are not too high and wages which are not too low for the encouragement of consumption. It is about time we manifested a little gratitude in the labor market: gratitude for the high standard of living we enjoy, the skillful workers, the resourcefulness of our industrial system when it works in unity. And about time we expressed that gratitude dynamically through the manifestation of good will.

This Thanksgiving will be a thoughtful time. It had better be.

Originally printed in The Christian Science Monitor, *November 17, 1945.*

Horn of Plenty

Minnie Klemme

If I had a horn of plenty to fill,
    I would take from the field, take from the hill.
I'd not spare the garden its green and gold;
    I'd ask of the bee; I'd ask of the fold.

Just so does our God, who has mouths to feed—
    For the world is hungry, and all have a need—
As He gives us water and sun and air,
    Supplying our wants with infinite care.

I do have a horn of plenty to fill,
    By lending a hand and doing God's will
All through the summer and into the fall—
    When the first leaf reddens, the last geese call.

May God's horn of plenty fill to the brim
    And a day of Thanksgiving be held for Him.

Handmade Heirloom

Mary Skarmeas

**STENCILED TABLE RUNNER WITH BATTENBERG LACE. Stencil by Lisa Thompson.
Photography by Jerry Koser.**

STENCILING

I never imagined that the lovely burnished gold stenciling that decorates the backs and struts of my thirty-year-old Hitchcock chairs had such a long and varied history. On the wall of a cave in Lascaux, France, a prehistoric man left an imprint of an outstretched hand filled in around the fingers with colors from the earth. His primitive signature, a natural stencil, reveals an innate need to create and communicate, to leave something behind that says, "I was here." The simple art of stenciling has served this need throughout human history.

The art of stenciling—that is, applying ink, paint, or dye in a cut-out design over a piece of paper, fabric, or any other material—may well have originated accidentally. One theory based on early historical accounts tells of a woman on the South Pacific island of Fiji who used banana leaves with cut-out designs as stencils to decorate bark cloth. The holes on the leaves, it is believed, were caused by insect larvae eating through the young, rolled-up leaves. As the leaves matured and unrolled, they revealed a distinctive pattern of holes—a ready-made stencil!

Throughout the centuries, people in every walk of life have used the art of stenciling to adorn their houses of worship, their homes, and their clothing. Buddhist monks in China in the seventh century stenciled sacred texts on temple walls, a practice that helped to preserve their religion since the stenciled texts withstood the ravages of years in the damp climate far better than other manuscripts. At this same time, Japanese craftsmen were using stenciling to create designs on fabric and paper. In Europe, the art of stenciling evolved from its basic form into a beautiful and practical art. Stenciled depictions of Bible stories were used to decorate the walls of churches and to teach illiterate church members. Modest home owners who could not afford canvas paintings were able to decorate their walls with stenciled art.

As one good idea led to another, stenciling was adapted to every kind of surface imaginable. In America, early settlers who were forced to leave behind the beautiful furnishings and fabrics that had added so much pleasure to their lives found stenciling to be a means of adding some color and design to their rustic new accommodations in the stark New World. With creativity fired by necessity, they produced original designs to cover fabric, walls, furniture, and other household objects.

During the early part of this century, the art of stenciling declined in its decorative uses, and stencils were most commonly used to mark crates, boxes, and road signs. The modern decor of our homes became pristine and monochromatic. Walls were left neutral—painted white or some shade of off-white as background to furniture and accessories. Wallpaper, which had been favored for some time, began to go out of style. The emergence of border wallpaper during recent years has drawn attention to decorative walls once again, and stenciling has come back into favor as an easy, inexpensive way to add color and personal taste to a room's walls and furnishings.

Stenciling is now widely popular. In response to this renewed interest, kits have become available that contain everything necessary to decorate a room, a piece of furniture, or anything else. You can find ready-made patterns in almost every design imaginable. And today's methods of applying paint are simple and neat; so anyone who wants to try stenciling should not hesitate due to lack of experience.

Books can offer step-by-step directions and sometimes come with several popular designs that you can copy. Craft books feature many projects for decorating fabrics—place mats, table runners, and napkins with seasonal patterns; children's sweatshirts; Christmas tree skirts; sheets, pillowcases, and coverlets. I have even seen books with designs for an entire, coordinated bedroom, from the stenciling around the doorways and windows to delicate stenciled edge work on the pillowcases and coverlet. As for design and color, use what is readily available, or get your inspiration from your own taste or from nature. The shapes of leaves, fruits, and vegetables and the colors of the varying seasons provide excellent choices. If you are a beginner, start small and simple. Stenciling a design of autumn leaves or pumpkins on the ends of a linen table runner or on the corners of a place mat will not only give you the confidence to go on, but you will have a one-of-a-kind, hand-crafted item that will bring pleasure every time you use it.

I have seen in the homes of friends and relatives amazing and beautiful ways of using stenciling. My niece placed a row of pineapples across the wall over a window instead of a valance. She also decorated a large plain wooden chest with various leaf and flower garlands—a unique and special hope chest for her daughter. Sunrooms, with their many windows, are brighter and cheerier with colorful borders around the doors and windows. An eager stenciler could add simulated plates around the room above a plate rail. Stenciled mock tile can create the same effect—it's not only beautiful to look at, but think how much easier to maintain!

One of the beauties of stenciling is that if you don't like what you've done, or if after a while you tire of the design, there is no messy wallpaper to remove; just paint over it and start again. But when you have done something you like, just as the prehistoric man who left his handprint on the wall of the cave in France, you have created something distinctly your own, added a touch of personality to your home, and said "I was here."

Mary Skarmeas lives in Danvers, Massachusetts, and is studying for her bachelor's degree in English at Suffolk University. Mother of four and grandmother of one, Mary loves all crafts, especially knitting.

A Thanksgiving Day Prayer

Mamie Ozburn Odum

This day, dear Lord, on bended knee
We bring our humble thanks to Thee
For this homey spot, this house, this roof.
These gifts we know are ample proof
Of Thy great love and daily care,
Giving plenty with some to share.
No words that ever have been said
Express our thanks for daily bread,
For strength in life we daily cleave
To merit gifts that we receive.

This day, dear Lord, most reverently
We bow in humble thanks to Thee
For minds to think, to work and plan
And live in peace with our fellow man.
Thank Thee for tasks to bake and mend,
For comfy fires for which to tend,
For every home that is like these
We thank Thee, Lord, on bended knees.
Giving thanks for love and living
We humbly thank Thee for Thanksgiving.

48

COLLECTOR'S CORNER

Lisa C. Thompson

REDWARE PLATE. Pennsylvania. Courtesy Winterthur Museum.

AMERICAN REDWARE

I've always wanted an antique wooden sideboard in my dining room filled with interesting and colorful handmade pottery. I can picture the diverse array of plates, platters, covered sugar bowls, and pitchers carefully arranged among the gently aged shelves. It is not an unreasonable dream, considering the multitude of choices in collectible ceramic pottery. With its rustic good looks and unique decorative possibilities, American redware is one type of pottery that many ceramics collectors find particularly charming.

The most universal definition of redware is any earthenware pottery created from red clay. All earthenware pottery is porous and is fired at a relatively low temperature. Examples of redware have been found in many different countries and dating back several centuries. Egyptian redware goblets and jars have been discovered that date back to the fifth century B.C. In America, Native Americans were perfecting redware pieces long before Christopher Columbus set sail for India, and the potters at the Santa Clara Pueblo in New Mexico are still known today for their stunning redware pots.

The term *American redware pottery*, however, usually refers to a specific category of naive, utilitarian pieces widely used along the Eastern seaboard from the seventeenth until the mid-nineteenth centuries. Redware potters usually established their shops and kilns directly on a site of common, red earthenware clay. The potteries, which were often family establishments, were sometimes combined with brickyards since the same material was used for bricks and roof tiles as for the various plates, cups, jugs, and jars that were needed by every household.

Since direct access to the rich, red clay was crucial, redware potteries were often scattered throughout the developing countryside. Most potters sold their pieces by wagon within a limited area near their shops. Redware is easily breakable; so the pieces could not survive being shipped long distances.

Most redware examples originated in the eastern part of the country, although pieces have also been found in Texas, Utah, and California. By far, the most important state for both sheer quantity of redware production and ingenious decoration was Pennsylvania. Pennsylvania potters are undoubtedly best known for their use of a decorative technique called sgraffito. Also called scratched ware for the method of creating it or tulip ware for the frequency of that floral design, sgraffito features a scratched design through an opaque slip. Slip is a thin liquid clay used to decorate or coat ceramics and to which different coloring oxides were often added. Immigrant potters who traveled to the New World naturally imitated patterns from their native countries, and the sgraffito decorations on Pennsylvania redware often resemble the decorative certificates called frakturs that were popular in the Pennsylvania German culture.

Since redware was pottery at its most primitive and was primarily intended for daily use, especially in the early days of America, colors and decorations were necessarily limited. Therefore, most redware pieces received a simple lead glaze for protection and waterproofing. Many collectors prefer the more colorful and ornate examples of redware. To novice collectors this presents a false impression that most pieces were many-hued and decorative.

Because redware potters worked with limited resources, pieces were usually left their natural reddish-brown color. For more colorful pieces, manganese could be added to the glaze to produce a dark brown or black shade; copper oxide for green; and yellow oxide for yellow. Pieces covered in only clear lead glaze were sometimes strikingly mottled or streaked from varying kiln temperatures or impurities in the clay. Sometimes colored slip was trailed or dribbled on the object for a decorative effect. Writing words such as "Apple Pie" in script on a pie plate—a process known as slip writing—was also popular.

While redware potters were limited in their decorative techniques, wavy lines, geometric patterns, and simple drawings such as birds were sometimes scratched into the clay's surface before firing. Metal punches were used to impress more complicated images such as a rosette. The earliest redware potters tended to imitate Old World designs such as copying the inscribed pattern on a silver English teapot. But with time, American craftsmen began to develop their own unique style.

Redware pieces were almost never marked by makers. Any redware that is marked is usually worth more to collectors. While educated guesses can be made as to an unmarked piece's place of origin, all such guesses should be viewed with healthy skepticism. When potters moved to a new job in a new community, it was customary for them to take their tools and designs.

While almost all redware pieces, such as plates, jugs, and bean pots, were thrown at the potter's wheel, redware items have been found that were hand molded. These distinct pieces offer variety and whimsy to a collection. A surprising array of pieces were made, including such interesting articles as redware doorknobs, inkwells, doll house furniture, washboards, and birdhouses. Some collectors choose to focus on certain types of pieces, those from a particular region, or pieces with specific decorations, such as slip writing or sgraffito.

An article in *The Pennsylvania Mercury* in 1785 warned readers of the ill effects of using lead-glazed pottery. The article stated that the lead glaze "is imperceptibly eaten away by every acid matter, and mixing with the drinks and meats of the people, becomes a slow but sure poison." Despite the admonition, redware was still produced throughout the nineteenth century, but to a lesser extent. At the same time, salt-glazed stoneware, a stronger and safer product, was steadily gaining in popularity.

Collectors enjoy their redware pieces as display items only, since the lead glaze makes the pieces unfit for drinking or eating from. Although stoneware may have replaced its predecessor for utilitarian purposes, redware retains its charm as a favorite slice of Americana.

Lisa C. Thompson gleans additions to her own eclectic collections every time she scouts out another yard sale, flea market, or antique shop.

November on the Shore

Gladys Cooper Cole

The wind is blowing cold and harsh;
 Its sting is chilling deep
And sweeps across the bay and marsh
 To where the dunes are steep.

Now that the frost nipped all the green,
 Tall grasses have turned brown.
At weathered docks and lanes between,
 Small boats are all tied down.

The mounds of swaying, brown sea oats
 And wind-shaped yaupon trees
Are like a fleet of fishing boats
 Tossed by the stormy seas.

But wind-tanned rugged fishermen
 Load nets, and all agree
To cross the sound and brave the wind
 And take their boats to sea.

November now is in her prime
 Since Summer closed her door,
And Autumn dots the coast with hues
 That lead the men to shore.

CAMDEN HARBOR
Maine Coast
Gene Ahrens Photography

HEATHER R. MCARTHUR

AMY CHENEY BEACH

In an age when accomplished composers and musicians were mostly European, Amy Cheney Beach arose as not only a great American composer, but one of the premier female composers of the late nineteenth and early twentieth century. Beginning at a surprisingly young age, Beach worked diligently to create a distinctly American genre of music while retaining elements of the classic European style. Her lifetime efforts led her to become the first American woman to compose a symphony, and she left a legacy of chamber music, piano pieces, and symphonies which are now being rediscovered as valuable pieces of the American musical tradition.

Amy Cheney Beach was born on September 5, 1867, in Henniker, New Hampshire, to parents Marcy and Charles Abbott Cheney, prominent New England citizens and leaders in the papermaking business. A precocious child, Amy's exceptional talents were recognized as early as age one by Mrs. Cheney, an amateur singer and pianist and Amy's first teacher. Amy was able to sing numerous tunes on pitch by age one, improvise and memorize long strands of music by age two, and by age three she had taught herself to read. When Amy was four, the family moved to Chelsea, Massachusetts, where she insisted on formal piano lessons and began composing basic waltzes. At her first public recital at age seven, Amy performed pieces by Handel, Chopin, and Beethoven and was declared a child prodigy.

Mr. and Mrs. Cheney were encouraged to send Amy to study in Europe where she could receive the most prestigious instruction. Her parents, however, elected to send her to a private school in Boston where she studied piano under such renowned composers as Ernest Perabo and Carl Baermann. Remarkably, Amy had only one year of formal training in harmony and composition.

At the young age of seventeen, Amy Beach made her debut with the Boston Symphony. Her performance of Chopin's *F Minor Concerto* prompted one critic to write, "Thoroughly artistic, beautiful, and brilliant performance . . . with a totality of conception that one seldom finds in players of her sex." Years later, Beach's *Gaelic Symphony* would become the first piece by a woman to be played by the Boston Symphony.

Soon after her debut, the teen-aged Amy married Dr. Henry Harris Beach, a widowed physician twenty-four years her senior. Dr. Beach had significant musical knowledge himself, and Amy once stated that her husband joined her mother to become "the kindest, most helpful, and most merciless critics I ever had."

Her happy yet childless marriage allowed Beach to devote all of her time and energy to composition. As in earlier years, she developed a rigorous course of study for herself and continued to push her musical abilities by composing large-scale works. In 1892, her ambitious *Mass in E-flat* premiered at the Handel and Hayden Society in Boston and established her as a major American composer. Soon thereafter, Beach was commissioned to compose what became a widely praised piece for the Women's Pavilion at the Chicago World's Fair.

From her early years at the piano, Beach, as an American and a woman, yearned to create her own distinct style of music. She did not limit herself to incorporating her own Anglo-Saxon heritage into her music. Instead, she experimented with Native American rhythm and melodies and was heavily influenced by folk tradition.

Beach made her first trip to Europe in 1911 where she spent four years performing and working diligently to cement her reputation as an awe-inspiring composer. Highly praised in Germany, Beach demonstrated her musical genius to European composers and pianists who were now her counterparts. At the end of a successful tour, Beach returned to the United States where she spent summers composing in New England and winters touring until her death in 1944.

Beach left a definite mark on American music. She opened a path for others to follow through both her accomplishments and her support of all musical endeavors. She held leadership positions in several musical associations, and she often hosted musical soirees in her home where she not only performed, but also encouraged developing composers and musicians. Her enthusiasm and sincere dedication to the art she loved only heightened Beach's popularity with the public and the critics, a popularity which continues to this day.

It has been said that as a child Amy Cheney Beach thought of piano keys as colors, mixing and matching to create a beautiful landscape. After reflecting on her lifetime of musical success, it is obvious that Beach was truly a gifted artist, adept at creating masterpieces from her piano's palette.

A native of Louisiana, Heather R. McArthur is a recent graduate of Vanderbilt University, where she majored in religious studies. She worked as Ideals' editorial intern during her senior year and dedicates much of her free time to volunteer work.

My Autumn Treasures

Alice J. Christianson

On hazy autumn afternoons
When all the fields are brown,
When Mother's making chili sauce
And Father's gone to town,

I like to wander down the lane
Through rustling aspen groves

Until I reach the vineyards where
I find my treasure troves

Of perfumes, rare as any found
On Araby's far shore,
Embodying for me the scent
At Autumn's pulsing core.

She casts her jewels around me
As far as eye can see,
Bright purple, red, gold, amber-brown—
A priceless tapestry.

No other season has the power
Through sights and sounds and smells
To permeate my senses and
To work such subtle spells.

I should be sad as summer slips
So silently away;
Instead I feel enriched by yet
Another autumn day.

An Autumn Wonderland

Loise Pinkerton Fritz

It's an autumn wonderland
    With shades of vibrant hues:
Russets, yellows, reds, and golds
    And skies of cloudless blue.

Front lawns decked with painted leaves,
    Some raked in towering piles;
Pumpkins sitting everywhere,
    All carved with happy smiles.

Corn fields to be harvested
    With cobs all hanging low;
Roadside stands with bright displays
    Of harvest's bounty-flow.

It's an autumn wonderland
    Where vivid color reigns
With beauty that is so intense
    It sets the soul aflame.

BOUNTIFUL HARVEST
Pownal, Vermont
Dianne Dietrich-Leis Photography

A Quail Tale

Carol Hogan

When I went down the road
    To collect the early mail,
I saw in front of the bushes
    A family of strolling quail.

Father came first, The Protector,
    Trailing three little ones in a row,
Followed by Watchful Mother
    With one more baby in tow.

In single file they proceeded,
    Each nodding and bobbing its head,
And I could hear flutters of sweet talk
    Though I couldn't discern what they said.

I quietly spoke, "Good Morning!"
    And my voice had a friendly edge,
But they took my words as warning
    And disappeared under the hedge.

Five long, silent minutes they waited,
    Hiding themselves from sight.
I stood motionless by my mailbox,
    Hoping they wouldn't take flight.

At last, with soft, sudden stirring,
    Father's top knot peeped out;

And the trio again filled the footsteps
    Of their captain, their leader, their scout.

From her camouflage Mother sped forward
    Into the golden sunshine.
But, oh, did she know, I wondered,
    That baby wasn't in line?

They made not one backward glance
    As they quickly marched away,
Thinking only of empty tummies
    And the simple routines of the day.

Should I search for that smallest fellow
    And set him out in plain sight?
Would he call to his mother and father,
    Or would he be speechless with fright?

In an instant, in frantic flurry,
    The tiny quail made timid sounds;
That same moment the Nervous Mother
    Stopped and turned around.

This time she walked him before her,
    Making sure he heard her reproach,
And soon they caught up with the father,
    Their captain, their leader, their coach!

WINTER SHELTER—BOBWHITES
David A. Maass, artist
Courtesy of the artist and Wild Wings, Inc.
Lake City, Minnesota

A SLICE OF LIFE

Edgar A. Guest

BOARDING THE BIRDS

I run a boarding house all winter long
    For quail and pheasant and the sturdy sparrow.
The pay I ask is just a bit of song
    And, lest this life of mine shall grow too narrow,
A glimpse of something different now and then
    From cold, bleak highways peopled thick with men.

At dinnertime come in the hungry birds
    To find the corn spread out as on a platter.
They tell me nothing in so many words.
    They eat and leave without a lot of chatter;
Yet that white ring around the pheasant's neck
    Is quite enough to pay the dinner check.

Sometimes I think how bare this life would be
    If never songbird happened by to cheer us,
If, being human, ostracized were we
    By every other creature living near us.
We'd get along somehow beyond a doubt!
    It's pleasanter to have the birds about.

Edgar A. Guest began his illustrious career in 1895 at the age of fourteen when his work first appeared in the Detroit Free Press. His column was syndicated in over 300 newspapers, and he became known as "The Poet of the People."

Ode to the Red-Headed Woodpecker

Beverly F. Walker

My Feathered Friend, you seem so gay
While stopping by for seed today!
Quarrelsome has been your trait
As on the feeder's edge you wait

To fuss at birds that come and go
And claim the treasure yours alone.

Your boisterous and busy way
Has slowed me in my tracks today.
I realize the gift that's mine
In seeing you drop in and dine.

You leave no tip; I leave no bill—
Just come back to my windowsill.
In counting blessings, you are one
I thank God for when day is done.

Thanksgiving Song

Hilda Butler Farr

For every gift that comes our way—
A bird that sings, a child at play—
For all the lovely fragrant flowers
And for the friendships that are ours,
*   We thank You, God.*

For every dream across the years,
And memories of smiles and tears,
For songs that lift the heart from care,
Companionship that we may share,
*   We thank You, God.*

For home wherein we turn for rest
To find the ones we love the best,
The liberty for which we stand,
And peace that lies upon our land,
*   We thank You, God.*

From My Garden Journal

by Deana Deck

CHRYSANTHEMUMS

To mention the word chrysanthemum is to call up images of lavish centerpieces on food-laden Thanksgiving dinner tables; cool, crisp football weather; and colorful corsages festooned with ribbons in school colors. When I was growing up, my dad used to take the family out to football games occasionally. Most were high school games on Friday nights, but the really exciting ones were on the Saturday after Thanksgiving. I'll always carry with me the image of my mom wearing her blue coat with the mutton sleeves and a large yellow mum corsage that had been delivered by the florist. She always brought the corsage home after the game and saved it in the refrigerator for days—I'm not sure why. Perhaps it was too beautiful to throw away, or maybe my mother simply hoped another occasion to wear it would arise. Once, in fifth grade, I talked her into letting me wear it to school. I was the center of attention until the petals started dropping off!

Although today's mums are inexpensive and available everywhere, they once were reserved only for the aristocracy of Asia. In fact, in Japan it was once a capital crime for a commoner to possess a chrysanthemum.

The plant originated in China. One legend tells of a boatload of twelve boys and twelve girls of the royal court who were sent on a quest to find a sacred herb that would sustain the life of the revered emperor. The voyagers carried with them basketfuls of golden chrysanthemums to trade for the life-giving herb.

Before they had gone very far, a terrible storm blew up, washing them ashore on an unhabited island in the Japanese archipelago. As their boat was sinking, they salvaged their belongings and the baskets of mums. Marooned, they settled in and created a dynasty. One of their first acts was to plant the mums.

In 910 A.D., the first Imperial Chrysanthemum Show was held, and the emperor named the mum the national flower of Japan. The mum wasn't democratized in Japan until after World War II. During the war, the emblem on the Japanese flag that became so familiar to Americans, and which many still think is a rising sun, is actually a sixteen-petaled mum, the emblem of the *mikado*, or emperor.

The mum made its way to America in the mid-eighteenth century, but it wasn't until 1902 that the Chrysanthemum Society of America was formed. At that point the mum was strictly a conservatory plant that could not withstand cold winters or hot summers. Breeders worked to develop a plant that would be hardy enough for the garden. They

CHRYSANTHEMUM

were busy! C. Elmer Smith introduced some four hundred varieties in Michigan and Alex and Rod Cumming of Connecticut transformed the plant into the garden mum popular today. One Cumming contribution was the introduction in 1932 of the Korean hybrid mum—the spectacular "football" corsage bloom.

Today, mums can be purchased for as little as two or three dollars for a four-inch pot. One of the most reliable of these garden mums is the Yoder's Prophet series available at many local garden centers and large discount stores.

Chrysanthemums are photoperiodic, meaning that they bloom in reaction to the short days and cool evenings of fall. Greenhouse mums that are in full bloom in spring have been tricked into thinking it's fall by being kept in a shaded hothouse where the length of the day can be controlled.

Mums come in a bewildering array of colors and types. Colors range from yellows and whites, to reds and bronzes, oranges and pinks, lavenders and purples, and my favorite, grenadine, a coppery pink shade. In addition to the familiar pompon type, there are anemone types whose daisy-like blooms have a large central disk and a large ray of petals. Spider mums have long tubular ray petals coiled or hooked at the ends. The thread varieties, straight tubular types, have fewer petals than typical mums; and the spoon varieties feature tubular petals that flatten out at the end like tiny salt spoons.

Chrysanthemums are easy and economical to grow. They are not bothered by pests or disease, and in most parts of the country they are perennials, returning with more blooms each year. They require full sun and ample water in hot, dry weather. Plant them in rich, well-draining soil and mix peatmoss or leaf mold into the soil. Feed the plants in spring with a general purpose plant food with a formula of 5-10-5. Repeat the feeding in mid-July to give the plants a good dose of nutrients before they start to bloom.

To help your plants develop a bushy habit and lots more blooms, it's important to pinch the tops off the plants whenever new shoots are four to six inches long. Cut or pinch back the tops of this new growth by one-half to one inch. This step will cause the stems to branch and form more buds.

Mums have the ability to form buds over a long period of time, but the first buds will wait until the others are ready before opening up. Pinching helps this process go smoothly. As long as new branches are being formed, the early buds will remain closed.

To protect your mums in winter, give them plenty of water during the dry days of October to send the roots off to rest all plump and juicy. In cold climates the plants can be pruned back in spring, but in warmer climates it's better to prune them in the fall, as they may continue to grow through the winter.

After the ground begins to freeze, mulch the plants well to prevent them from being heaved out of the ground during thaws. Use leaves, straw, peatmoss, or compost. In spring, cut back old stems and remove the mulch so the soil will warm up. By fall, your mums will reward you with beautiful blooms.

Perhaps the chrysanthemum is America's favorite fall flower because of its hardy nature and its colorful brilliance in October gardens. I still find myself wanting to keep my mum corsages until the last petals fall free. Perhaps I'm trying to hold on to my favorite fall memories of Thanksgiving dinners and long-ago football games where mums always played a special part.

Deana Deck lives in Nashville, Tennessee, where her popular garden column is a regular feature in The Tennessean.

Purple Asters

Charles P. Isley

In harmony they sway and dance
Down any shady lane;
In corner nooks of stubbled fields
They mourn the vanished grain.

The frosty breezes jostle them
In carefree autumn fun
As off across the countryside
Their lacy blossoms run.

They cluster by a singing brook
Or by a meadow pool
To nod at their reflections
In the waters, clear and cool.

Oh, flowers of springtime beckon me,
And summer's blossoms call,
But autumn's purple asters are
The fairest blooms of all.

NEW ENGLAND ASTER
Aster novae-angliae
Pacific, Missouri
R. Todd Davis Photography

White Chrysanthemums

Patience Strong

Far into November when
The fogs are thick and gray,
The lovely white chrysanthemums
Their perfect blooms display.

Pure as snow and pale as clouds,
And yet our glance they hold
More than all the gorgeous tones
Of bronze and red and gold.

Startling in their wintry whiteness,
Restful to the eyes,
After all the brilliant colors
Of the autumn dyes.

Nature, ever provident,
Has paused to scatter here
White flowers for the burial
Of the departing year.

The Happiest Days

Douglas Malloch

Sometime someone very old,
Walking somewhere, east or west,
With a hand to which to hold
And a cane on which to rest,
Suddenly will stop and gaze
All around a little while
And will say, will say and smile,
"Here I spent my happiest days."

Someone sometime, maybe you,
Thus will come upon a spot,
Come upon a place you knew
That you never have forgot.
Though your back perhaps is bent,
You will straighten up a bit
And will say, beholding it,
"Here my happiest days were spent."

Sometime somewhere, maybe now,
We are living life the best.
Care may furrow someone's brow,
Grief may sadden someone's breast,
But you yet may backward gaze
Down the road you walk today;
And to someone you may say,
"Here I spent my happiest days."

The Harvest

John M. Packham

The dormant land is white with snow,
    And fields are now at rest.
The harvesting is over, and
    The soil gave us its best.
Tall grew the corn with summer's sun,
    With summer's wind and rain,
But now the frost is neighbor to
    The stalks that still remain.
The pumpkin is not on the vine,

EVENING LIGHT, MILKING TIME. Steven R. Kozar, artist. Courtesy of the artist and Wild Wings, Inc., Lake City, Minnesota.

No apples on the tree,
And winter's cold has changed the scene
From what it used to be.

The harvest is the end result
Of all that had been planned,
And we with nature witnessed it,
The giving of the land.
The fallen leaves of autumn are
Asleep against the ground,
And only winter's beauty is
A thing that can be found.
We give our Pilgrim-type of thanks
For many, many things
That must include the miracle
A harvest always brings.

The Unraked Leaf

Tom McFadden

Bright, solo leaf, now unpursued,
Seems ember in time's interlude.
Surviving, shiny autumn flake,
Missed by early winter rake.

Fallen brightness, salient,
Briefly lengthens season spent,

Its wondrous hues a last contrast
To the chilled and fading grass.

A moment cast of special sun
Throws glitter in a rainbow run—
Resplendent flash of magic brief
In final spell of unraked leaf.

EARLY FROST
Mark Twain National Forest, Missouri
R. Todd Davis Photography

Autumn Passes Too Soon

May Smith White

When poets write of seasons,
 They mostly write of spring;
But I like best to write of fall
And the harvest it will bring:

October's high, blue heaven,
 The yellow fields of grain,

The blending of the goldenrod
Before November's rain.

And then the rain of autumn
Mellows the ground once more
 Beneath the fallen leaves
 That carpet autumn's floor.

Readers' Forum

Meet Our Ideals Readers and Their Families

ATTENTION *IDEALS* READERS: The *Ideals* editors are looking for "favorite Thanksgiving memories" for the magazine. Please send a typed description of your favorite Thanksgiving memory or family tradition to: Favorite Thanksgiving Memories, c/o Editorial Department, Ideals Publications Inc., P.O. Box 305300, Nashville, Tennessee 37230.

Has your faith in God changed your life in a remarkable way? We'd like to hear your story. Please send a typed description to: Stories of Faith, c/o Editorial Department, Ideals Publications Inc., P.O. Box 305300, Nashville, Tennessee 37230.

MARIA DADE sent us this photo of her two sons, Benjamin, age five, and Matthew, age one, who are shopping for pumpkins on a beautiful October day. The Dades welcome the opportunity to venture each autumn to Schartners Farms near their home in Kingstown, Rhode Island, to pick pumpkins, sip hot apple cider, and enjoy the outdoors. Pumpkin carving on Halloween Eve has become quite a tradition for Benjamin, Matthew, and their father, Christopher Dade. Matthew is anxiously awaiting the day when he will be able to "trick or treat" with his dad and brother!

BONNIE HOKENESS of Adrian, Minnesota, shares this charming picture of a rainbow above her farm after a storm. The beautiful landscape provides a perfect spot for Bonnie and her husband, Ray, and their crops of corn and soybeans. The extra space also comes in handy when the couple's large family of four children and eight grandchildren comes for a visit!

FAYE FIELD of Longview, Texas, sent *Ideals* this photo taken recently at a family reunion. Pictured is her great, great-niece Whitney Muller, age ten months, clinging to her favorite cousin, Faye's grandson Tommy Samuel Field. Tommy, age seven, enjoys the attention from his baby cousin, and, fortunately, reunions are frequent.

Grandmother Faye told *Ideals* that her family is a close-knit group of people representing all generations. Even though relatives are scattered throughout Texas, they are able to see each other as often as once a month. Faye is an avid *Ideals* reader and has given most of her family members subscriptions throughout the years!

THANK YOU Maria Dade, Bonnie Hokeness, and Faye Field for sharing with *Ideals*. We hope to hear from other readers who would like to share photos and stories with the *Ideals* family. Please include a self-addressed, stamped envelope if you would like the photos returned. Keep your original photographs for safekeeping and send duplicate photos along with your name, address, and telephone number to:

READERS' FORUM
IDEALS PUBLICATIONS INC.
P.O. BOX 305300
NASHVILLE, TENNESSEE 37230

ideals

Publisher, Patricia A. Pingry
Editor, Lisa C. Thompson
Copy Editor, Michelle Prater Burke
Electronic Prepress Manager, Amilyn K. Lanning
Editorial Intern, Heather R. McArthur
Contributing Editors, Lansing Christman, Deana Deck, Russ Flint, Pamela Kennedy, Patrick McRae, Mary Skarmeas, Nancy Skarmeas

ACKNOWLEDGMENTS

BOARDING THE BIRDS from ALL IN A LIFETIME by Edgar A. Guest, copyright © 1938 by The Reilly & Lee Co. Reprinted by permission of the author's estate. THE HAPPIEST DAYS from THE HEART CONTENT by Douglas Malloch, copyright © 1926, 1927 by Douglas Malloch. Used by permission of the author's estate. WHITE CHRYSANTHEMUMS from THE ROUND OF THE YEAR by Patience Strong, copyright © 1948 by E. P. Dutton & Co., Inc. Reprinted by permission of Rupert Crew Limited. Our sincere thanks to the following authors whom we were unable to contact: James J. Metcalfe for DAY WORTHWHILE and May Smith White for AUTUMN PASSES TOO SOON.

GIVE A GIFT FROM IDEALS THIS CHRISTMAS

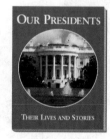